ANIMAL BRIDE

ANIMAL BRIDE

Sara Quinn Rivara

**TINDERBOX
EDITIONS**

Tinderbox Editions
Molly Sutton Kiefer, Publisher and Editor
Red Wing, Minnesota
tinderboxeditions@gmail.com
www.tinderboxeditions.org

Cover artwork by Daria Hlazatov, "Tiger's Bride," 2013
Cover and interior design by Nikkita Cohoon

for Jonah, always

Contents

I.

II.

III.

Animal Bride

You must be a small, fierce animal.

I.

Lake Ice

The length of a first marriage: eternity. Shore-fast ice
creeping onto the Lake. In such cold, when told to sing, stones

fell from my throat; when told to sit still, knees hum.
So the Lake chews the pier when told to stay quiet, sand

runs in frozen ridges up the dune. It's all done; the mouth
unfolds its origami cranes. Was I the wife who cowered

in bed? You can't sing with a broken neck. That girl folds
her hands into steeples: the open door, crowds

in rabbit-fur hats. Winter knocks its elbow against the window
glass. When told to stay still, terns jab the horizon's

barbed line. For years I thought the sun couldn't
shine: smudge low in the sky. Water a cold sludge. The child

who clung to my side and cried. White pine and grouse
and woodcocks and their upside-down brains undid daylight

in ropes, darkness braided my hair. But winter-shocked
frogs will resurrect. But what cannot be unspoken:

hell. Beneath the floe, the depth of water: miles.

Once Upon A Time

The bride had no heart, just a clock that ticked away the hours.
  A field
of bloody flowers. The place where the zipper sticks, the skin
  unmakes;
a naked woman in a bed of snakes. Lonely turnip. Ham-hock,
  stone. Oh,
just say it: the best woman is a silent one. Marriage a clot.
  Cutlass moon
against her throat. Cupboards filled with mice. Her long hair
  glimmered
with rice. Did she leave her shoes by the door? She did. The
  mute swan
sings in the reedy pond. Red flowers wave their dangerous wands.

Upwelling

The truck stopped in a pile of leaves, engine
heaving. Girls up the road; one looked
back. Someone sawed off all the branches

of the Bradford pear. A million ladybugs
where he got out of the cab, lit a cigarette.
The soft roll of flesh over the waist-

band of her jeans, empty sky, a sharp whistle. Tall
man bent, single flower out of season,
sharp wind over the snow-struck field, bees

clustered around the cells and the queen asleep.
The girl stepped over a slushy puddle; starlings ate
all the seed-corn. The queen dreamed of clover,

sweetbread, honeycake, dead alewives
on the January shore. Wind raced over the water,
cold rose (like smoke) and the hem of her dress tore

in the slammed door; he turned radio to static.
Horizon, an arrow,
and the water tobacco-brown.
Cleft in the earth
where hell broke through:
flowers bloom in ash.

Lacuna

I was a happy wife
the way I was happy to see
the little red flower bloom
on the crotch of my panties
at thirteen, and when he said he
loved my body but not
my mind he said
it was a joke but I knew
white silk makes a bridal
shroud and the morning
I was thrown against
the wall he said he thought
I was the dog—oh,
whatever can be fucked
is expendable
and here where
he's parked the car
and tries to press
me into the ground I know
this was always a cemetery
though we called it
a park, all the graves
unmarked and any
woman with a man's
hand on her throat
knows how it feels
to be the loneliest
person on
earth.

The House Where

This is the house where I killed a squirrel with a pellet gun. I was nine months pregnant. This is the wall with a fist-shaped hole. I knew all the names of the weeds: chicory, pokeweed, purslane, vetch. Me. The neighbors never came outside until the septic failed and the police came because of the stench. The wife was carried out dead. Then my baby came. The dogs patrolled the halls and the baby slept in my bed. The man threw me against the wall. He said he thought I was a dog. The baby threw up blood. Weeds overcame the garden. And then, and then. It isn't safe to say: leave. Hope. No. Sky marled with birds. The baby chewed my breasts. My fever rose. Western sky streaked red.

Birthright

The light beneath the door flickers
as the night nurse walks the hall

and the baby sleeps on my chest though
we're not allowed, and he's gone

home to drink, and I shrink to a pin
and from the open window smells of rain,

honeysuckle, earth. So this is death: love
so fierce it burns the heart to slag. The baby's

puckered face floats in that flame-blue light
and will I be okay if the baby takes my life?

The Lake batters the beach.
The sky rags a hole. What if the answer

is no.

Letter from the Underworld

Sometimes I think you've forgotten me here
in this small house, snow piled in grey heaps
by the door, snow drifting like fallout past

the windows. Even the birds have stopped
coming to the feeder. The house smells of marijuana
and mildew and the baby chews my breasts.

My body has become borderless; there's a blank
spot in the middle, pool with black flowers, red
of the dead swan—a woman is empty

space, closed mouth, broken jar. Blood in the baby's
milk. The baby cries and I sing
and drive to the grocery and act like I'm alive

and the swans unravel. Turnip, cabbage, lamb:
each hour loses a name. Dishwasher, diaper, ash,
ash, ash. It's cold in hell this time of year. What I was:
disassembled. Snuffed out just the same.

Lake Trash

What we give to the Lake she throws back: syringe, condom, fishing line, shotgun shell, teenagers dead after diving off the pier. The bottom is invisible until it breaks your neck. All those years spent on dirty sheets, Budweiser, cheap weed: if I tell you exactly how it was, I'll get it wrong. He'll say that I lie, *you always were a crazy bitch.* My bride price was a life pushed beneath the waves, wedding dress a net, baby a ballast weight. Even now I'm afraid. The horizon's a blade, a match, a brand. Alewives wash up dead and rotting on sand.

Deserves It

Twilight flickered behind the house
with seventeen mismatched windows,

unlocked fence. A whistle, leaves burning,
the smell of charred meat. *Girl, whatchu got*

in that stroller? Baby you want to suck
my dick? The sky was a blank.
The trees were scars. Girls are from Venus, the devil

in bars. In a barrel a small fire burned
the windows lit orange. He sucked air

between his teeth, his shining head, hand
on the open gate. My baby reached

toward flowers that vined between links:
morning glory, bindweed. The man licked

his lips, tongue an adder, an asp. I pushed
the stroller further down the street. The gate creaked. *Baby*

I know what you want. I know where
you live. In his hand, a penknife gleamed
around his head the starlight streamed.

> *I know what*
> *to do*
> *with a woman*
> *like you.*

Boylan Street

The children came over the landfill. Six or seven hard-eyed boys. The only girl let her dog run ahead, slipped her hand into mine. The boys stayed behind. She was missing three teeth; hair a white sheet against her colorless cheek. The boys talked low, kept pace. In the stroller my baby slept, face pink and slack as sunset. The children followed me for blocks: landfill, abandoned mill, pinestand. At home all the lights were off. And I. My husband cleaned his guns. The boys carried a switchblade, a rope, a bottle of cheap scotch. Above us, the Milky Way flickered on, off. The baby opened his eyes and mewed. *Are you going home?* the girl wanted to know. Her dog's name was Zion Becoming. In the sky, buzzards flew.

Three Dogs

A house made of tarpaper, plywood. A blue tarp
snapped on the roof. Children swung from trees.
Three dogs on three gold chains. Chicory in spurts, wild

carrot, hogweed. A miracle none of us went blind. Mosquitoes
and blackflies. Turkey buzzards spun giant circles over our heads
and crouched on the mill's ragged edge. May flumed into June

and the river algae bloomed. And the apple trees threw down
their sweet perfume. By the time of tornado season, one of the dogs
was gone. A fresh heap of dirt beneath the apple tree, dust devils,

cicada-dust sky. The river soured, Charon's skiff stabbed weeds.
The other dogs blinked clouded eyes. The baby had three milk
teeth. He chewed. I bled. And the next day another dog chained

to the tree chewed black-furred bone that stuck from the soft
earth. And hogweed bloomed against chain link. Sirens, hail,
wind. Cerberus at the gates. My baby shut his split-pea eyes.

Around us the dust began to rise.

How to Write a Poem

Begin with what hurts: tornado weather, cold front, waterspout.
With the empty bed, field of narcissus and the ravine so dark

it could cleave a girl clear in two. Boylan Street sunk in landfill
gloom, tree of heaven clicking against window in the living

room. The baby never sleeps. So name the birds, baby chewing
your breast: wren, titmouse, nut-hatch, buzzards by the dozen.

A pair of sparrows on the back stoop, little brown nothings. A
bruise like a rose. Cracked tooth, water bill, fucking. Even so,

the crabapple blooms and smothers the yard with sweet perfume.
Even so, a robin weeps in the dwarf cherry: *storm,*

storm, storm. Without language, a hole, a chute, a woman's
mouth sweet as rotten fruit. Sewn shut. The song dwindles,

ends. Thunder. Begin: *I, ache, gouge.* Begin with singing.

Say nothing, you're dead. Begin with the names of the girls
who got out.

To Persephone

The sun hung from a noose
and all the blackflies were swarming
did he say you had an affair (did

you wish there was an affair) did he
set the neighbors to spy, say he'd take
your son, all the money

if you lawyered up, say he'd
take an ax and chop
you to bits? It was a life

you had before, books
beach rose, glacial drift,
a trip to the coast, did

you get it back? Tell
me what I've read isn't
true, tell me you didn't

return and if you felt
his hand on your neck, if
you watched your son's

furrowed face disappear
behind the window of his rusted
truck, that you grabbed the boy

and ran. Tell me you will stand
with me upon the rim
our babies pressed to our breasts

and never go back.
That all those years in hell
taught us to fly.

II.

Forest Avenue

This is a woman in a bikini. This is a hamburger,
condom left on the bedroom floor. Children
wild as raccoons. The sky wide as the space between
a woman's thighs. On the corner of Forest Avenue
a girl lay down behind the forsythia, a line
of boys waited their turn. We watched and sucked
our fingers for salt. Girls drunk on Listerine in the culvert.
Years have burned between now, then. I married,
divorced. My son says whore when he means horse.
I wipe the dirt from his cheek. A woman's body
is edible as ground beef, elderberry, wild
onion in the overgrown creek. Pliable as rendered
grease. Along the highway Johnson grass clutters
the ditch, sumac, syringe, dead ash. Everything burns.

Wet Dream

A river, oil slick, electric eels. Warm water, turgid, brown as sewage, as a song sparrow singing from the marsh edge. The Great Dictator in his grey jumpsuit motors up, the boat gilded with cherries. Sunglasses, two peat fires, two blank mirrors. A sheep's stomach stuffed with doves. Trees scrabble up the inky bank. The sky an aborted blue. Eels snap live wires at my feet. The boat lists and the motor trails a winding sheet of exhaust, oil, weeds, cassette tapes, women's hair, cabbage roses, columbine, the Shroud of Turin sewn into a wedding veil. *Don't you love me?* the Great Dictator asks, his small fist at my throat. My ass round as a cantaloupe. Eels flicker like dwarf stars. The rush of black wings. He tries to flick his cigarette onto the turf. He drools on his polyester shirt. Pompadour catches the sunset like a postcard: *wish I was never here.*

Jesus, My Briar Rose

The sun a fractured dinner plate on our first date. I swallowed
you whole from Pentwater to Petoskey, Route 31 made straight
through the wilderness, your breath a balm on my burned

flesh. Yet, the dogs of my attention are whimpering, *love.*
And you're somewhere else, flame-tongued. I followed
your robe until I went blind, until paralytic they lowered me

through the broken roof and you kissed my soft breasts. My sick-
ness left: that womanliness. And now that we're finally alone
it's getting serious. You sent me notes, crowed three times

in the summer dusk, licked dust from my feet like sugar. Unlock
your tongue and speak my name. Magdalen. Unclean. Hamstring
your hungry heart. The valves of my attention open to your sour

longing and heaven-handled, naked, I do as I
should. Keep my mouth shut. Unhinge. Mud. But I'll out-
last you, sweetheart, though I'm caught, in your net of air,

of loss, of blood.

The Gospel According To

Last night I watched my friend die. Her children couldn't cry,
she eased away like water leaches through loam, or blood
turns to water turns to wine: don't you see? Nobody

here is fine. Nobody offered you a drink when you finally
stopped by and scooped the drear world to your chest. The hurt
aren't the blessed. The world so empty and it still can't float.

You were off with the boys again, cruising the Meijer parking
lot looking for sinners, the never-saved and no time for us. *It's
best this way,* you crooned. *My father's house has many rooms.* Heart-

soft bastard, you were late. And this morning, my arm
against your breast, my thigh against your thigh, my tongue
against your flesh—yet. Grief wells up, it swells the floors

and gums the gears. All I can taste is the salt of your sweat:
snow in swales. Sure, I'll believe
you're mine. I'll lie. Let me caress your pretty sacred head.

You tangle your fingers in my hair. You lick, you
moan. You rise to raise the dead.

After You Left God, I

prayed tongue and breast wither, go straight
through the roof, ascension's sweet conflagration—but
the fallow field of soybeans beaten by light cry: autumn.
Cleaving. I thought I was left, but I meant: leaving.

Birdsong through cleft trees. And when you
return riding that little white pony, circus tent billowing
behind you like hellfire, your beard grown to your knees
and swaying in the rapturous breeze, rime will climb

all the windows and the elephants will bolt from the cars
and the train will jump the tracks right into my soft
lap. *Sweetcakes,* I'm going to say, *I've made you a cup
of tea. I've woven a terrible rug on my loom. Hold*

the shuttle. Start the clocks. Time scaffolds its bony frame
against the horizon: tree and electric lines. Red as a fox. As
the apple left in the compost pile, the steady line of ants
that carries it all beneath the dirt. I've set my watchfires, sweet.

If you come back, I'll be ready. I'll be the first beast you meet.

Infidelity

A rope of smoke rose from the garden all night
and a fireman pounded the door near four. The roof

was afire and was it I who lit the match? It was,
wasn't. A woman's body can fit between mattress

and wall, can fold around her husband's dick like a dumb
doll. The air is grim in late fall, and everything loses its wits

to the wind. Sassafras, hickory, swamp withering dry.
What was the future but a dead bird? The Devil stoked

the stove with wormy wood. If I screamed, someone
would hear. But I didn't, should. I unlocked the door, I

invited him in. Black hair curled
on his apple-shaped head. But I'd already baked

the fruit into a pie, I'd already sugared the plums, cut
the branches from the dying tree. I was the snake,

he the flea. He undid my dress, his mouth poke-
berry red. The baby slept in his little white bed. The Devil

smelled of wet earth. The Devil smelled like cold rain. I kissed
the backs of his knees, the cup of his throat. He undid my.
Again—

We ignored the clocks, the baby slept on. We burned
that house to the ground.

Sand

It was the summer the sand came, the summer it filled the house, blew in through the cracks, between my teeth. The summer the cicadas changed their tune: two notes to one. Drone and thrum. The birds undid their bodies like bombs. Storms came every day. Sand between the sheets, the towels, in the curve of my back, clogging the drain. Something died and I killed. It tried to kill me. Sand filled my mouth. I choked on the gold. The air furred as black bear, and the baby held his breath. I held him to my chest. Here is the choice: leap or drown. Some girls can't fly. The Lake swallowed up the Pleiades. Against the shore, waves broke their small backs.

Road to Canaan

The boys lit the cherry trees. The can knocked against their knees and the hill was steep and the orchard sung with bees, or screamed. The boys lived in three green houses down the street. They were eleven, or ten. Their fathers gave them the idea. Their fathers lit the match. It hadn't rained in weeks. Wind like an arm across their necks. And the cherry trees doused in gasoline burned. And blossoms fell like wings. I followed them, though I was not dressed, though my baby slept. And rust flecked swords guarded the garden. The angels in their dirty fatigues fell and kissed my bare feet. I undid the stays of my— And my nightgown muddled and ruined. Ruined us all. The baby was half wolf, half bird. He wept in my arms. The baby's mouth like an open wound. Green weather on the wind. Land of Milk and Honey. Over the Lake, the stars were clotted cream.

Selkie

I found my seal skin in a locked drawer. He kept the loaded gun by the back door. Wolves, he said. Men who wouldn't hesitate with a woman like me. For safety. What he meant was to know my place. What man ever saved me? I could taste salt in my mouth. Cormorants wheeled the shore. The pelt felt stiff. In the mirror my face a wax mask. My son already furring behind his ears. He slept in my arms. I drew the skin over my head. I locked the doors. I took my boy to the edge of the cliff. Swells broke. We leapt. Salt-light. Anemone. Limpets. I heard gunshots from the shore. Listen. Living takes such courage.

Sleeping Bear Dunes

Let me tell you the story of the bears, Sugar, how they ambled down the dune one afternoon and ate all the honey, all the bread. How they sniffed the top of your pretty little head. Undo your mouthful of thumbs. They buried all the guns and bathed their skins terrible in the cold waters of Lake Michigan. Which skin did you take off and fold on the sand? The female one. The one that did us in. The human girl who undid her life like a shirt's torn seam, that scar, that hurt. The sycamore dangles its empty hive. Of course it would come to this: such conflagration. The future presses its meaty snout against our narrow throats—can you feel its sour breath? Pine and wind. Put on your wild pelt. Open your mouth.

Animal Bride

The cherry trees burned, blossoms fell like snow. Beach roses withered as the Holy Ghost grew like autumn olives in my throat. The dunes moved four inches east. Lamprey sutured their mouths to lake trout. The sun a broken egg. And my teeth were stars. All around the house, the sand gathered its skirts, gold hummocks, gold hills. The baby's skin soft as Lake-in-June. He attached, a lamprey to my breast, drew blood. And the crows brayed all afternoon in the sycamore snag. Sand came and filled the first floor and the second and the third until all that remained was roof and I lay naked on the soft tar. The baby's mouth a dry rose. And the fires overcame the orchard. I once had an animal skin. Look: let me show you the scar.

Bitch

The rain stripped all the trees down to the bone, then
came snow. The Straits lapped up the beach like a dog,

Beneath the bridge, Lake Huron foams.
Route 31 a mist: dunegrass, wilderness.

The stars beat the Straits with their tiny fists.
I heard the door slam. My name, shouted.

My name, profane. Did I really think
I was a he-owned thing? The beach grows cold

beneath my feet. My throat raw from all this singing.

Orchard Fire

The cherry trees were already dead. So why not gasoline, why not burn? The baby wailed. My head split. And all those years in hell spilled out. There was a woman with the head of a deer, a girl who pulled a fish from her throat. Three doors nailed shut: Opulence, Terror, Wish. The Lake beat her head against the headlands, mergansers pulled out all the trout. My son, my stone. My tongue a bird, my spine a hanging rope. The orchard licked with flame. Whatever you think I did, I did. Whatever god unhinges its jaw and swallows me will choke. I tore out my life with my own hands.

III.

To Press the World Against my Chest

-after Li Po

In Kalamazoo, this final winter, January's watery light soaks
the yard; berm, fallow garden, bare elm, ragged oak.

Snow melts off the roof in torrents before freezing overnight,
another three feet of snow off the Lake. The schools stay

shuttered, roads full of slide-offs, abandoned cars. The Lake
freezes for miles. Last September, a deer stumbled

into the yard, drunk on windfall apples and the reservoir woods
wool-dark, shot through with fireflies. Cicadas played violins

high in the trees. News is brief, Li Po says,
and heaven never ends—

the Midwestern horizon stretches away, rubber band, slingshot,
winding sheet. The snow covers all the evidence:

what kept me here, what let me go.

Thanksgiving

The fields empty, yellowbrown, carcass of a deer in the barrow
ditch and his great-grandmother's house half-heated, salami
with peanutbutter dip and raw shrimp and his uncle brought

meth and his bobcat Bob and wolfdog Ronald Reagan and his
uncle's wife tried to make me buy her homemade candles made
with human teeth and they would cook me a tofurkey because

aunt with mushrooms growing out of her head and me
were the only vegetarians and that in itself was an act of terror
but I wouldn't eat it because they wrapped it in bacon

and after my divorce it was toast and wine alone
in the apartment and woodswalk snowpath and lake-falling-from-
sky and my son clinging to my arm as his father dragged

him into his truck and drove off, his nails in my skin drawing
blood and when as kids before all this we'd go to my grand-
mother's house of twenty aunts and uncles and thirty-three

grandchildren and an eighteen-hour-old salmon on the counter
and chess pie and someone would find Uncle George's cocaine
and someone else would flush it down the drain and it's not

surprising the choices I made and then we'd all go bowling
and my dad would get drunk and smoke Marlboro Lights all the
way home with the windows rolled up and I'd rub a circle

in the windowfog and outside there were men pulling a deer from
the ditch, her bloated stomach her blackblank eyes into the bed
of their rustedblue pickupand my sisters and me

in the backseat in a cloud of yellowsmoke pinching each other's legs until they puckered until they bled.

Madonna of the Dry Tree

The tree is a crown of thorns. The fountain
a stagnant pool. There is a man with a gunnysack
in the woods—wearing a gold ring. He knows
my name. Oil on his tongue, oil on my head.
Mosquitoes whine. Without its purple fruit
the tree is scaffold, noose. Every god takes
what he thinks he's owed: firstborn son, virgin bride,
potable water turned to wine. I fold my hands like a bird,
bite sharp my tongue. He picks his way through
my dead Eden; acorns, rotten figs, bone-
meal stuck to the bottom of his shoes. A mother is root,
sky. A woman is shell, cage. He raises his arms, coronas
his head like a scar. He the rose, I the thorn.
I hold our baby like an egg, red welts rise
on our soft skins. Bloodflower blooms by the gate.
Waiting among the dead leaves, a black snake.

Dead Reckoning

My boy earthquake, licked finger in the light
socket of the universe, catapult, tornado weather.

My boy kerosene, beach pea, blue egg in the briar
patch. Nebula, twitch, crane in the shorn field, snow

choked hillock and cliff. The Straits frozen solid, a chain
of Christmas trees all that ties us to the mainland.

My boy the wind squeezed through a closed door, rocks
beneath the bridge, the sway, the bend, his face behind

the dirty windshield of his father's truck as it pulls away
into a storm, the roads unplowed and crows huddled

in the sycamore. My boy the schooner, the Great Lake
barge, dappled, disappeared grayling. The steel bridge

erased in the snow, the little iceboat whose sails unfurl,
catch wind, and I the ice, so thin, so thin.

Mater Terribilis

I wash you in saltwater, my fish-boy, my silver swimmer. I keep the door locked. In the room where. In another room your father rolls a joint, drinks beer, watches porn. The ocean water warms, grey-formed. Fish grow large and improbable. Fish with antlers of a deer, the face of a crying boy! In my arms you sleep, my compass, anchor, rope. Hope: a byssus thread. The father pulls me down by my hair. The father knots the nets. The father wants me dead or his. He put his knife to our scales. Bruised my cheek. You turn to me in your sleep. I will kill, maul, burst the sea wall. Unpin the sky from the earth. My body, undo, undo. All this I'd do, my boy, for you.

The Swan Girl

This isn't the calm before, not storm, not rope dangled over the
pier to the swimmer too bold for her own good. Not the drowned
girl but the swimming one. The one whose mouth is red and
open, teeth like the bleached shells of zebra mussels that litter the
beach after every thaw. There is rain coming. Black line over South
Manitou Island. This is the garden dark and the sky ruined with
light. Sin like it doesn't matter. That's the ticket. That's the grit
between her teeth.

                                              Meanwhile, the earth tilts
toward erasure. Meanwhile the pier is buried beneath a shelf of
ice. Two wedding dresses, a veil with sturgeon embroidered in
the hem. A room filled with someone else's things: model trains,
Commodore 64, half-filled saucers of cream. Take everything.
The snow has gone soft at the edges. The girl folds her wings and
sings: the old life calved from the floe. Her son turns to her in his
sleep, tucks his feet beneath her hip. Snow falls and falls outside
the window and the Lake crumples at the edge, lacy dress matted
with sand, with ice. The headless swan. The girl who swims and
swims.

The Mermaids

When I was a girl, your mother will say, *the river was cruel and burned your clothes away.* But she swam every day. Her fingernails turned grey. She was our girl then, until the world closed in: lipstick, dry land, a man. Together we made you. Tonight her weeping waked you. There are men outside in sleek dark cars. They have your name on a little white card. They won't let your mother up the stairs. They smoke expensive cigars. She'll keep them busy, her mouth raw and her skin: thin. Open your window. Knot your sheet into ropes. You can stay, or climb down. All the birds sleep; the river is cold. We must breathe water or we will drown.

A Wilderness of Women

*And the woman fled into the wilderness, where she hath a place
prepared of God, that they should feed her there a thousand two
hundred and threescore days.*

—Revelation 12:6

A milksnake curls around the throat of a woman in a milkwhite
dress. Her knees mud-scabbed her mouth a bouquet of stitches
finger pricked, three drops of blood on the spindle, the thorn,
     the razor

blade dropped on the garden path   there are other
girls in the woods who have stuffed their mouths with sweet-
bread mushrooms   who have scaled the tower with gun-

powder beneath their nails hair snarled with burrs, blood
children strapped to their backs and knives to their thighs
manna, salamander, heart-root.

The riverwater churns cold. White sheets bloom with roses
of blood. What if the story is a thread, a wire, a snake, a rope
that moors the flat-bottomed boat to the bank and the water

is dark and filled with eels? Girls with their mouths sewn shut
tongues cut   wedding cake stuck to the roofs of their mouths
clamber in   dresses translucent with rain.

Untie the knot, cut the rope. The dragon opens his grimy eye.
Snake, speak:

The boats choke the stream, so
many more come.

In the wilderness hunger gathers its cloud
like the point of a storm touching down.

Speak, Snake

All summer apples
and honey. She held her boy
and me in the sun
on her soft lap. Months
without pain.
Now the garden heavy
with sweet fruit, he's
come back. He tries to wrench
the child from her lap. Do you
hold it against me if I move
so quietly not even the mice
can hear? If I slide beneath
dead leaves, raise
my head and strike
his heel.

After (Grace)

Humility tastes of apple, tampon, worm. Woman without her
pelt. *Hailmaryfull* until he was done, every window shut. Is
there someone crying? There is someone crying, someone

bleaching the sheets. Self, damned ghost. What if there was no
birth? no way out? It would've been easier if he. It would've
been easier if some-

one'd believed. Weak-kneed. My boy throws his arms around
my neck, sleeps curled against me, his long body like a wolf
beneath the sheets. Will he look like his father, cruel-edged
face of a sword. He smells

                    of turned earth, apples. Will he know his
mother, splayed and trussed like a deer on the bed, how I
prayed for deliverance, poison, any sharp thing? My guilt.
How still I stuck.

        Bird, be a curled fist, flint, wish.

My body a suit of armor, a small fish. Cicadas seventeen years
                                    asleep and pissed.

The Midwest's belligerent hot dish. Sometimes, no one stays
behind and all that's left is the smell of cooking, a broken
cup.

Grace: a funeral shroud. The body: a gold.
The woman in the tower knots sheets into ropes. Not princess;

witch. I took my boychild and carried him. Beneath his tongue
the eden seed: my tree bears dangerous fruit. All names slough
off or claimed by rot. I claim this bed, this heat, this wont.
   The women

who climbed before me sing. They've carved out the woodman's
   heart.

My body: unexploded star. A fool scar. Warm wet spot.
Is the cleft where the baby tore. Is lightning, the spot where your
   mouth. O, love-found-late: an ocean map.

                              Unclothe

me, salt anemone. The moon unscrews her blistered eye.
Has it been one life or two?

Bird, be gasoline, scree, the mountain's burning tree.

The moon is soused. When she touches water, she'll clean

                                     us out.

Lilac

I want to be touched. I learned. In your
apartment, air dry and warm, Portland-
grey mist outside and our bodies lepidopteral—

the small filaments of my stomach, thigh, my wet
wings—basal, discal, postdiscal, submarginal—though
we could fly, we are earth-rubbed. Spitshined. Sheets

slick with it. Back in Michigan, late winter lingers,
scrapes away the stars, moon a bleached turtle shell.
But here two ravens preen on the gravel roof outside

the bedroom window, lilacs swell with new
bloom. For this, Pan chased Syringa through the wood;
for *this:* coffee percolating in the kitchen, books

open on the table, I'll eat the apple, all of it. My leg
against yours, hand on your chest: a closed
flower. Thirty-five years and I thought myself

impermeable but for the weight of my son in my arms.
You taste like lilac, violet. You move against me
wing against wing, all flight, all clap-and-fling. 2,000 miles

away my son wakes into our old life, calls me across
the Continent: *Mama.* We are leaving, we are leaving
small bird. My world trembles at the welted edge:
this is the song of. The salt of your kiss.

Mercy Then

A great horned owl calls
across the arboretum; stuck

in her cage, left wing broken
and healed at an angle. Does

she still dream of flight despite
all the white mice she can eat

and none of the uncertainty
of the autumn field? It is cold.

Snow holds off, but the clouds
swell. Catbirds cry where

the nets are tied, branch to branch.
You hold my hand and kiss.

There are holes in the nets;
birds stream the evening sky.

Second Marriage

Play house with me, Sugar. Let's Braille the bed
with our bodies, kill the rooster and bake him into bread.

We'll watch snow crumple the potter's field, crows
like blood stains, dune grass flat and grey as ash.

The windowglass grows cold; snow squalls over the Lake
clamber thick-legged over the waves. Come back to bed. I'll

feed you saucers of milk, blood sausage, lake perch. The throat
is a highway, the lungs the Bride of Christ, the tongue

the rood. I, cup. Who am I to doubt the resurrection and the Life?
Snowfield, salt, skin. The laundry stiffens on the line.

—Unhinge me. Let all the beautiful, terrible things pour in.

Parable

This is the parable of the magnolia tree: in the morning it blooms and by evening it's shattered on the grass. Everything grows too fast. The Pacific rubs my neck. I put the vast grasslands, the iced-over Great Lakes between *us* and *then*—I came West. My new husband curls around me at night, all I could imagine of *miracle* and *wish*. Sunrise a broken egg, Mount Hood a flat white triangle in the East. Faith a bird that cleaves the clouds on a blear day. Faith a woman in a blue dress. A boy asleep in a field. A neck. In Michigan, a two-headed lamb pivots behind museum glass: that life, or this. I will not turn back.

Benediction

Bless the woman washing blood from the sink, the baby
with colic, the unmade bed. Bless invasive carp, river silt.
The stupid half-dead heart. It came apart. Bless the locked

door, the book; bless rosebush, bless cunt. The girl whose hair
snags on barbed wire, the animal chained to a tree. Bless rust.
Bless the boy and the broken window, bless his bleeding hands.

Bless the fur in my throat, cocklebur in the dog's wet
coat. Mouth, kiss me. Bless the scar, bless blood, bless
the stitch. Bless the goddamn god who doesn't exist. Bless

that bitch—where is the center, where is the *you* I've prayed
to every night since I left? In the wilderness. The only god:

animal. We're all we've got:
this little slit in the firmament that is—what? Meyou.

Everyone. All of it: dry rose, pinecone, wind through the gorge
sharp and wet. Our soft fur. Our babies, our bodies
pressed, river, rocks, cliff. Love

is a rending, I want to give.
This body, my bed, turned earth, damp woods,
my garden's gone to seed.
The madwoman cries like a wolf:

The attic is burning. The attic is fire.
The curtains flutter like doves.
Where ash—

The Thing with Feathers

Is kidnap, is clamor. Is the broke-down truck, is how a girl can be smart *and* fucked. Is salt, fir, moss. Is ocean, fire, my boy's feet tucked beneath my hip. A hinge, an edge. A woman's body is the selvage end, is the field where all things grow. A match tossed in the brush pile. Let it burn. Let the past collapse in a heap. To live with fear is a kind of death. My son shifts in his sleep, puts his head on my breast. There was once a tearing, a razor wire. Or it was my flesh. My soft girlskin a wedding dress. It was the rest of my life, torn out, flapping.

Sugar Sand

And when I did it I used a knife. The bird was my tongue. And I said *I'm done.* I slid it beneath my ribs and emptied the place the heart should be, and out came water and out came god-on-his-knees. And I used it to slice away my skin and let my pelt gleam in the terrible light; all the stars tumbled into the Lake. And I climbed the pier and leapt and the Lake was still as stone and I fell for years before I knew I'd flown. And the baby grew into a boy and held my hand in the damp lot and the lights flickered on. And my life was called Persistence, Regret, the Glory of God. And the boy held the rock split by fire in his palm. And light fell from the sky. And light rose in pillars from our feet. The dunes were whipped with wind and the sand sang beneath our toes and my son threw stones into the water—the high arc of blessing, future, wild beach pea that clings even in death to the fence. Lake lashed pier, drowned moon. Headland. All night. Oh, I'll burn this fire my whole life.

Acknowledgements

Blackbird "Lake Ice," "The Swan Girl," "Road to Canaan"
poemeleon, "Sleeping Bear Dunes," "After You Went God, I"
   "How to Write a Poem"
Midwestern Gothic, "Animal Bride" (winner of the Lake Prize)
Tinderbox Poetry Journal "A Wilderness of Women"
RHINO "Sugar Sand"
The Nashville Review, "The House Where"
The Fem, "Letter from the Underworld" and "Selkie"
Word Riot, "Mater Terribilis," "Benediction"
Devil's Lake, "The Thing with Feathers," "Wet Dream"
Split Lip Magazine "To Persephone," "Once Upon a Time,"
   "Forest Avenue,"
Tahoma Literary Review "Madonna of the Dry Tree"
Pittsburgh Poetry Review "Lacuna," "Boylan Street," "After (Grace)
   as "After Ever After"

For so many, I am so grateful:

Tinderbox Editions and Molly Sutton Kiefer who rescued my
book when it was orphaned, and to my editor Jenn Givhan who
helped me see my work in a new way.

All of my students who taught me more than I ever taught you,
who kept me afloat all those hard years. To my teachers who taught
me it was possible.

Corlyn, Joe, Abby, & Ben Schreck, and my found family in
Kalamazoo who held me when I couldn't stand, who helped me
go.

My Wally tribe.

Every singer and choir with whom I have performed: I could not write if I also didn't sing.

My sisters, Buddy, Katy and Anna, who taught me to be fierce. My parents who raised four girls to be animals.

Rob Yardumian, first reader, love, my partner in life. Thank you for making a new family with me. I love you always.

And to Jonah and Dashiell, who make everything worth it.

Sara Quinn Rivara's poems have been nominated for the Pushcart Prize and won the inaugural Lake Prize. She is the author of one previous chapbook, *Lake Effect*. Also a semi-professional classical singer, Rivara grew up in Chicagoland, lived for many years in Kalamazoo, Michigan, and now lives with her family in Portland, Oregon.